Synchronizing Souls: A Journey To Spiritual Awakening

Vidula Khanna

BookLeaf Publishing

India | USA | UK

Presentation by *BookLeaf Publishing*

Web: www.bookleafpub.com

E-mail: info@bookleafpub.com

ISBN: 9789360940607

First edition 2024

DEDICATION

To all seekers of truth and spiritual awakening,

May this book serve as a guiding light on your journey,

Illuminate the path to inner peace and wisdom,

And inspire you to synchronize with the soul's divine rhythm.

With heartfelt gratitude for your courage and curiosity,

This work is dedicated to your unfolding evolution.

May you find solace, inspiration, and liberation within these pages,

And may your awakening journey be filled with grace and profound insights.

Forever in the dance of existence,

With love and light.

Energising Reiki: The Dance of Energy

(Verses 1)
In the dance of energy, I find my way,
Through Reiki's touch, I come to sway.
From the Root to the Crown, I start to play,
Exploring the chakras, night and day.

(Chorus)
Energy flowing, through body and soul,
Each chakra spinning, making me whole.
With every movement, I feel the role,
Of Reiki's embrace, making me bold.

(Verses 2)
Rooted in the earth, the first chakra stands,
Sacral's flow, like water in my hands.
Solar Plexus shining, as I expand,
Heart chakra's love, spreading across the land.

(Bridge)
In the Throat, I speak my truth,
Third Eye opens, revealing my youth.
And to the Crown, I rise uncouth,
Transcending limits, in search of my truth.

(Outro)
So let's dance in the light of Reiki's grace,
In the rhythm of energy, I find my place.
Through the practice of Reiki, I embrace,
The power within, as I dance in this space.

The Alchemy of Liberation: Acceptance Journey

In the journey of liberation, a tale unfolds,
Of acceptance embraced, as the heart beholds.
Soul's growth in the dance of separation's art,
A journey of awakening, a transformational
start.

Eye to eye, acceptance meets separation's call,
In the crucible of life, where souls rise and fall.
Yet within this dance, freedom takes flight,
As we breathe in the glory of newfound light.

With each breath, we manifest our release,
From chains of illusion, we find our peace.
The air, so fresh, carries whispers of grace,
Guiding us onward, to a higher place.

Acceptance, the key to liberation's door,
Separation's gift, to explore and adore.
In this sacred journey, we find our way,
To freedom's embrace, where spirits sway.

Journey to Inner Peace: Awakening through the Sacred Silence of Spirituality

In whispers soft, the silence of spirituality
speaks,
Unveiling truths that heart seeks,
Beneath the noise of worldly din,
Lies the sanctum where spirits begin.

In the depth of silence, echoes rise,
Echoes of miracles, everlasting ties,
Binding us to all that's divine,
In the silence, we intertwine.

In solitude, the mind finds rest,
Amidst the turmoil, it's the best,
For in the quiet, the soul can hear,
The sacred whispers, crystal clear.

There's a rhythm in the quiet air,
A melody that souls declare,
In the sacred silence, we find,
The essence of all that's kind.

So let us seek the quiet within,
Where the sacred silence begins,
And in its depths, may we find,
The spirituality that binds.

Divine Haven: The Sanctuary of the Lord

In God's safe place, we find calm,
No worries there, just a healing balm.
With each prayer, we feel His care,
Guiding us gently, always there.

In His love, we're safe and sound,
No burdens weigh, no troubles around.
With each moment spent, we feel His embrace,
Finding peace and endless grace.

In God's haven, we find our ease,
A place of rest, a gentle breeze.
With open hearts, we come to adore,
In His sanctuary, we find much more.

So let's seek His shelter, clear and bright,
Finding peace in His loving light.
In God's haven, we find,
Divine love and peace, forever entwined.

Patience and Forgiveness: A Path to Peace

Patience and forgiveness, we must understand,
In life's ups and downs, they go hand in hand.
When troubles come, and hearts feel the strain,
Patience soothes, like a gentle rain.

Forgiveness is strong, it's like a key,
Unlocking peace, letting hearts be free.
When we let go of anger, let it be,
Peace fills our hearts, for all to see.

Let's wait calmly, let's forgive,
In this life we live, let's learn to give.
With patience and forgiveness, side by side,
We'll find joy and peace, far and wide.

Paradise Found: Finding Peace in the Lord's Heaven

There's a special place called heaven,
That's what I truly believe,
I'm completely sure,
About what this message means.

One night as I slept tight,
I felt my soul take flight,
Rising up from where I lay,
With arms raised up to pray.

I'm not sure why it happened,
It's a mystery to me,
But the feelings deep inside,
Were like my soul's decree.

The love I felt was huge,
No other love was near,
It was strong and mighty too,
Like it had always been here.

When my soul returned down,
To where my body lay,
A breath was all it took,
To make me speak and say...

"There is a presence of GOD"

Heart's Awakening: Embracing Growth

In healing's path, we discover,
Growth and grace, gentle and sure.
Like seeds in earth, we begin to rise,
Step by step, healing draws near our eyes.

Through good and bad, we learn to cope,
With love around, we find our hope.
In our heart's journey, wounds will heal,
With each new day, we find new zeal.

In easy and tough times, we learn to deal,
Love gives us hope, that's the real deal.
As days pass by, our heart will mend,
Each new day brings a fresh blend.

In the journey of healing, we discover,
That love and hope will never falter.
With every step, our spirits mend,
Finding peace that has no end.

Calm Waters: Sailing Towards Peaceful Horizons

In quiet waters, our boat moves slow,
Toward peaceful places where troubles go.
The soft breeze whispers, a gentle song,
Guiding us steady, all day long.

With each little wave, worries fade away,
As we head towards peace, in our own way.
The sun sinks low, painting the sky,
A picture of calmness, catching the eye.

In the ocean's hug, we find our peace,
The waves' gentle rhythm brings us ease.
No storm can stop us, on our way,
Peace is our guide, come what may.

So let's sail ahead, with hearts unfurled,
Towards peaceful places, in this wide world.
In calm waters, our spirits feel free,
Towards peace, we long to see.

God's Embrace: Finding Freedom in Detachment

In God's hug, we feel so light,
Free from things that end too tight.
With God close, we're never alone,
He's with us, His love fully shown.

Let go of stuff that comes and goes,
God's love stays, forever glows.
He's always there, his light so bright,
Guiding us through day and night.

Hold onto God, let others fade,
In His love, we find our aid.
With Him, we're safe, in His care,
Detached from things, but with God, we share.

Finding Calm: A Path to Mental Wellness

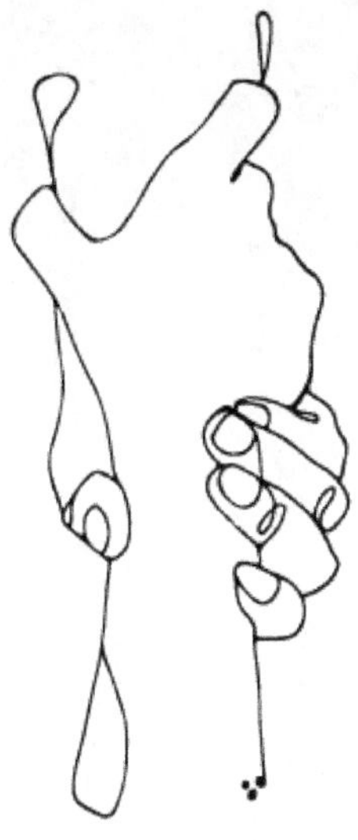

In the shadows where the mind does strain,
Lies a path to heal the pain.
With gentle words and caring touch,
We mend the wounds that hurt so much.

Through laughter shared and tears that fall,
We find the strength to stand up tall.
With every step, we move ahead,
Healing slowly, like a thread.

In friends we trust and love we find,
A soothing balm for the troubled mind.
With time and care, we'll surely see,
The healing of wounds, and hearts set free.

Sound Healing: Escalating the Path of Awakening

In quiet tunes, our souls find peace,
As melodies from pain release.
With every sound, a gentle grace,
Awakening spirits in every place.

With each vibration, hearts align,
In harmony, our spirits shine.
In sound's embrace, we feel the light,
Guiding us through the darkest night.

So let us listen, let us hear,
The healing music, ever near.
In simple words, its power clear,
Sound healing brings awakening near.

Yoga: Aligning Body, Mind, and Spirit

In quiet spaces, minds align,
A journey starts, transcending time.
With every breath, a sacred vow,
Yoga's path, here and now.

In gentle poses, bodies bend,
As souls awaken, hearts ascend.
Through sun salutations, spirits soar,
Finding peace on the mat's floor.

With every stretch, with every pose,
A deeper connection to life flows.
In union with the divine within,
Yoga's journey, where we begin.

So let us embrace this sacred art,
A spiritual journey, heart to heart.
In breath and movement, we find our way,
Yoga's path, leading to light each day.

Guiding Light: Nurturing the Hope

In the depths of the soul, where shadows may
dwell,
Hope emerges, a radiant spell.
In spiritual realms, where faith takes flight,
Hope guides us through the darkest night.

With every prayer, with every chant,
Hope's gentle whisper, like a sacred plant.
It blooms within, amidst trials and strife,
A beacon of light in the spiritual life.

In moments of doubt, when faith may wane,
Hope reminds us, we're not in vain.
For in the journey of the soul's ascent,
Hope is the guiding star, ever-present.

So let us hold onto hope's gentle flame,
In the spiritual journey, it's not the same.
With hope as our compass, our hearts ignite,
In the realm of the spirit, shining bright.

The Power of Hope: Lighting the Way Forward

In the tough times when things look dim,
Hope shines bright, breaking shadows grim.
Step by step, a new road appears,
Turning life to hope, calming fears.

From dark to light, from fear to grace,
Hope blooms strong in a wide open space.
With courage strong and faith as a friend,
Turning life to hope, till the very end.

Through challenges faced, and trials sore,
Hope's gentle touch leaves hearts wanting more.
In each struggle faced, we find a way to cope,
Turning life to hope, giving us scope.

So let's hold tight to hope's shining power,
Turning life to hope, hour by hour.
In hope's warm embrace, we'll always find a
way,
Turning life to hope, come what may.

Soulful Affection: Embracing Spiritual Love

In the quiet heart, a love so deep,
Forever close, forever to keep.
Spiritual love, a treasure rare,
A secret shared, beyond compare.

In the soul's depths, where silence lies,
Spiritual love, it fills the skies.
It goes beyond, it reaches far above,
Unveiling the secret of spiritual love.

In moments calm, in moments dear,
Spiritual love whispers, drawing near.
It heals the hurt, it makes us whole,
A love eternal, to nurture the soul.

So let's hold tight to this love divine,
The secret of spiritual love, yours and mine.
In its embrace, our true selves we find,
In the heart's sanctuary, love intertwined.

Prayer's Healing Touch: Nurturing the Soul

In whispers soft, in hearts sincere,
The power of prayer, forever near.
It reaches out, beyond the skies,
A sacred song, a soul's sweet cries.

In moments still, in depths of need,
Prayer's gentle touch, a faithful seed.
It lifts us up, when we're brought low,
A guiding light through winds that blow.

In times of joy, in times of despair,
Prayer's strength surrounds us, everywhere.
It connects us to the divine above,
A bond of love, an endless love.

So let us pray, with hearts sincere,
For in prayer's embrace, we find what's clear.
The power of prayer, a gift so grand,
Guiding us gently, hand in hand.

Radiant Paths: The Essence of Spiritual Enlightenment

In the quiet corners of the mind, a truth does
reside,
Enlightenment's whispers, forever untied.
It speaks of unity, of oneness divine,
Guiding us to realms, where the soul can shine.

In the heart's sanctuary, where wisdom lies,
Enlightenment's essence, it never dies.
It leads us to the depths of our being,
Where the soul's song, forever freeing.

In the stillness of the soul, where peace does
reign,
Enlightenment's presence, it does sustain.
It invites us to dance in the cosmic flow,
Where the seeds of enlightenment, forever grow.

So let us bask in its radiant glow,
Enlightenment's grace, to truly know.
In the dance of life, let our spirits soar,
For in enlightenment, we find forevermore.

Aromatic Grace: Discovering the Essence of Spirituality

In the garden of the soul, a fragrance so sweet,
Spirituality's essence, in whispers discreet.
It lingers in the air, like petals unfurled,
Touching the senses, transforming the world.

With each step we take, its fragrance surrounds,
Embracing us fully, where peace abounds.
It speaks of unity, of oneness profound,
Connecting us deeply, to all around.

In the fragrance of spirituality, we find,
A connection divine, to the eternal mind.
It lifts our spirits, it sets us free,
To dance in the light of eternity.

So let us embrace this fragrance divine,
Let it weave through the tapestry of time.
For in its aroma, we find our true worth,
In the fragrance of spirituality, we find rebirth.

The Heart's Companion: Embracing Friendship with God

In the whispers of the wind, in the rustle of the
trees,
God's friendship whispers softly, carried on the
gentle breeze.
In the laughter of the stream, in the twinkle of
the stars,
His friendship embraces warmly, healing all our
scars.

In the beauty of the earth, in the wonders of the
sky,
God's friendship surrounds us, ever present, ever
nigh.
In the warmth of the sun, in the coolness of the
breeze,
His friendship envelops us, bringing us to our
knees.

In moments of triumph, in moments of despair,
God's friendship holds steadfast, always there to
care.
In the highs and the lows, in every twist and
bend,
His friendship remains constant, a love that will
never end.

So let us cherish this friendship, a gift beyond
compare,
In God's loving embrace, we find solace and
care.
For in friendship with God, our souls find their
home,
A bond that will endure, wherever we may
roam.

Offerings of Love: Exploring Sacrifice for God's Grace

In the silence of devotion, where love does
dwell,
Sacrifice for God, a sacred tale to tell.
In the depths of our hearts, where faith resides,
We offer our all, as His love abides.

With each step we take, with each vow we make,
Sacrifice for God, our spirits awake.
In the surrender of self, in the letting go,
We find ourselves in His divine flow.

For in sacrifice, we find our truest self,
A connection divine, beyond earthly wealth.
In the surrender of desires, in the letting go of
fear,
We find His presence here, always near.

So let us offer our lives, our love, our all,
Sacrifice for God, in His grace, we stand tall.
For in giving, we receive, in surrender, we find,
The eternal peace and joy, in His presence, we're
aligned.

Unbroken Path: Continuing the Journey of Spiritual Discovery

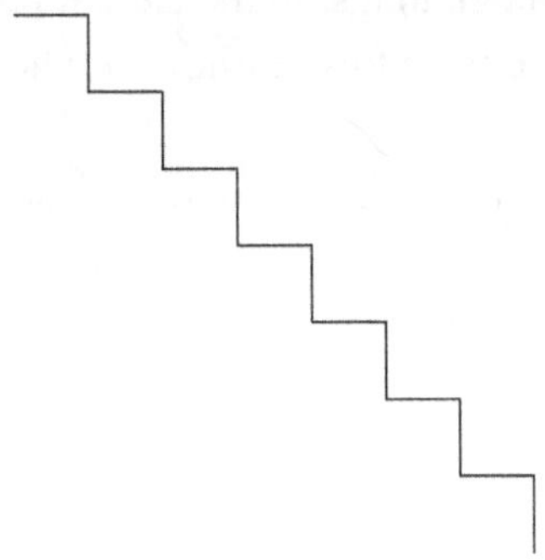

On the winding path of the soul, the journey
unfolds,
With each step taken, new mysteries untold.
Through valleys of darkness and peaks of light,
The spiritual journey continues, day and night.

In the moments of stillness, the whispers of
grace,
The spiritual journey continues, in every space.
Through the ebb and flow of life's ceaseless tide,
We journey onward, side by side.

In the embrace of the divine, we find our rest,
No longer searching, no longer stressed.

With each step taken, with each soulful glance,
The spiritual journey continues, in a timeless
dance.

For in the journey of the spirit, there's no end in
sight,
Only new beginnings, in the eternal light.
So let us embrace this journey with hearts wide
open,
For the spiritual journey continues, never
broken.

OM: The Sacred Symphony of Mental Peace

In the heart's quiet sanctuary,
A sound emerges, soft yet mighty,
OM, the ancient, sacred tone,
Its resonance is a healing throne.

In moments lost to endless strife,
OM breathes new hope into our life,
A sacred echo, deep and true,
A calming force that guides us through.

In the stillness, find your peace,
With OM, let all your worries cease,
A bridge to calm, a path of light,
Guiding you through day and night.

In the chorus of the stars,
OM resounds from near and far,
A universal song of release,
The sacred healing of mental peace.

Fusion of Worlds: Crafting Peace through Unified Energies

In the dance of earth and sky,
Where physical and mental lie,
A bridge of light, a glowing thread,
Connects the worlds where we are led.

The body's touch, the mind's embrace,
In this union, find a place,
Where thoughts and senses intertwine,
Creating peace, serene, divine.

In moments still, in movements fast,
The physical and mental cast,
A spell of calm, a sacred bond,
In their union, peace is found.

In this dance of form and thought,
Peace is woven, never bought,
A sacred aura, bright and free,
A beacon of tranquillity.

Tracing Smiles: Discovering Depths of Peace and Brightness

Track the smile that lights the face,
A gentle curve, a touch of grace,
In its glow, calmness found,
A radiant peace, all around.

Understanding, like the sea,
Depths of wisdom, flowing free,
Surface bright with laughter's glow,
Beneath, a peace that's sure to grow.

List the moments, pure and bright,
Understanding in their sight,
Depths of water, surface clear,

Hold the peace that's always near.

Track the smile, the calm embrace,
In brightness, find your sacred space,
Depths of water, surface bright,
In understanding, pure delight.

The Harmonious Flute: A Symphony of Mind and Melody

In the gentle breeze, a flute does play,
A rhythm soft, a bright ballet,
Proportional to mind's own song,
Where harmony and peace belong.

In each note, a world revealed,
Where thoughts and dreams are gently healed,
The science of its symphony,

Dances with the mind's decree.

Trip through harmonies, so precise,
In each sound, a sage advice,
The flute's rhythm, soft and light,
Dances with the mind's own sight.

Feel the rhythm, pure and true,
In its harmony, renew,
The flute's soft song, a gentle bind,
Proportional to the peace of mind.

Affirmations and the Soul: Weaving Positive Vibrations into Harmony

Affirmations whispered low,
To the soul, their truths bestow,
A symphony of hope and grace,
Binding heart in a soft embrace.

Positive vibrations hum,
Like a gentle, sacred drum,
Resonating through the veins,
Erasing sorrows, easing pains.

The soul responds with radiant light,
Transforming darkness into bright,
Affirmations lift and heal,
Revealing truths, profound and real.

Body and soul in unity,
Flowing with serenity,
With every affirmation's rise,
A surge of light, a new sunrise.

The Magic of Manifestation: Weaving Dreams into Reality

In the quiet of the mind,
A spark of magic we can find,
A thought, a wish, a dream to see,
The power of what can be.

With every wish, a seed is sown,
In fertile ground where dreams are grown,
Nurtured by the light of faith,
And watered by the path we trace.

Through faith and trust, the spell is cast,
Binding present, future, past,
In every moment, power lies,
To bring to life the dreams we prize.

Hold your visions close and tight,
With every breath, in day and night,
Manifestation's gentle hand,
Will guide you to a promised land.

The Flow of Light: Energy Between Hands

In the space between the hands,
Lies a force that understands,
A current swift, a vibrant stream,
Connecting us beyond the dream.

Palms aglow with gentle heat,
A meeting place where forces greet,
The energy flows, a river bright,
A testament to inner might.

Feel the warmth, the pulsing beat,
The magic in this quiet feat,
Hands aglow with power's touch,
A simple gesture, meaning much.

In this touch, a healing grace,
The energy finds its sacred place,
Between the hands, a force aligned,
A testament to power's kind.

Rivers of Serenity: The Sound that Soothes the Mind

The sound of flowing river's chant,
Through valleys wide and fields of slant,
It whispers secrets, old and grand,
To minds that seek to understand.

The melody, a timeless tune,
Underneath the silver moon,
It paints the mind in shades of blue,
With dreams that drift, serene and true.

Listen closely, you will find,
A peace that flows through heart and mind,
In every babble, every sigh,
The river's song will pacify.

The sound of flowing river's call,
Affects the mind, a timeless thrall,
With nature's symphony, align,
And find in it, your peace divine.

Love's Energy: Embracing the Soul with Understanding

Love, a symphony of energy,
That binds the soul, so tenderly,
In its rhythm, understanding grows,
Where hearts entwine and spirit flows.

Energy swirls, in vibrant hues,
Connecting souls, in joyful cues,
Love's symphony, a cosmic dance,
Where souls align in perfect trance.

Understanding, like a gentle breeze,
Navigates the heart with ease,
In its presence, conflicts cease,
Bringing harmony, a sense of peace.

Love the soul, with boundless grace,
Embrace its mysteries, in every space,
For in its essence, energy flows,
A dance of light where love grows.

Energy's Path: Exploring the Inner Currents

Follow the path where energy flows,
A journey within, where spirit grows,
Through chakras spinning, colors bright,
Connecting realms of day and night.

Embrace the flow, from deep within,
Where energy ignites the skin,
In every cell, a whisper heard,
The journey's map, a sacred word.

Feel the warmth, the vibrant glow,
As energy spreads, from head to toe,
A journey inward, to explore,
The essence of that forever more.

In harmony, the journey's bliss,
As energy and soul find kiss,
Embracing life's dynamic beat,
The journey's path, so bittersweet.

Flight of the Soul: Embracing Golden Light with Fireflies

Fireflies whisper in the night,
Teaching us to seek the light,
In the soul's depths, where dreams reside,
To let spirituality be our guide.

They teach us how to radiate,
The inner light that elevates,
To fly with wings of faith and grace,
And let our spirits interlace.

The human soul, a vessel pure,
Illuminated, steadfast and sure,
With each spark, it finds its way,
To realms where spirits gently sway.

Fireflies teach us to believe,
In the light our souls receive,
To fly with grace, with spirit's might,
And embrace spirituality's flight.

Divine Essence: Powers Within the Human Body

In the silence of the mind's embrace,
Divine powers find their place,
In the whispers of the soul's soft call,
Lies the power to rise and fall.

Through laughter's joy, through sorrow's tears,
Divine powers, dissolve our fears,
A touch that heals, a smile that lights,
Divine essence, in our sights.

Through eyes that see, beyond the veil,
Where truth and love forever prevail,
Hands that heal, hearts that mend,
Divine power, without end.

In every heartbeat's steady drum,
A connection to where we come from,
Human body, spirit's shell,
Divine powers, in us dwell.

Pathways to Authenticity: Seeking the Inner Self

Who am I, in mirror's gaze,
In reflections of passing days,
A silhouette against the dawn,
In memories that linger on.

Am I the echo of a name,
Or the spark within the flame,
Am I the silence in the storm,
Or the heart that beats, so warm?

Am I the echo of the past,
Or dreams that fade, too fast,
Am I the whispers of the stars,
Or scars that shape who we are?

In depths of silence, I aspire,
To find the truth, to feed the fire,
Who am I, in the endless sky,
In the boundless question, I fly.

Quest for Clarity: Unveiling the Purposeful Path

Along the path where dreams unfold,
The purpose of life, a story told,
In the beacon light, a steady guide,
Through valleys low and mountains wide.

Through doubts that linger, fears that bind,
The beacon light, a solace kind,
A compass true in stormy seas,
Showing paths where the spirit frees.

In its flicker, a promise made,
Of destinies where dreams cascade,
The purpose of life, in steps so bright,
Walked with courage, walked with might.

Let the beacon's light, in darkness glow,
In its brilliance, dreams aglow,
For in its gleam, the heart does know,
The purpose of life, where dreams sow.

Soul's Awakening: Unveiling the True Calling Within

Within the depths, where silence reigns,
The true calling of the soul remains,
An energy that pulses strong and clear,
Guiding us to purpose, drawing near.

Through the darkness, light does gleam,
A beacon bright, a hopeful beam,
Guiding us to where we thrive,
In the energy that's alive.

In every choice, the calling heard,
In whispers soft, in every word,
An energy that stirs the soul,
To find its purpose, to make it whole.

Embrace the inner self's true calling,
In every rise, in every falling,
For in its essence, we unfold,
The energy that makes us bold.

Air of Enlightenment: Chakra Awakening and Energy Flow

In the rhythm of breath, a sacred art,
The air and energy blend, impart,
Within the body's temple, a shrine,
Chakras open, in divine design.

Root chakra, earth's solid ground,
Sacral chakra, where desires abound,
Solar plexus, fire's bright flame,
Opening pathways, without shame.

Solar plexus, fires aglow,
Heart chakra, love's eternal flow,
Throat chakra, truths unfold,
Third eye chakra, visions untold.

Crown chakra, gateway to the sky,
Where spirit soars, without a why,
In the breath's ebb and flow, we find,
Chakras open, heart and mind aligned.

Strength in Every Breath: The Art of Deep Breathing

Deep breathing, an art refined,
Aligns with power, both heart and mind,
Inhale the calm, exhale the storm,
A symphony where strength is born.

Aligning breath with soul's intent,
Deep breathing's power, freely sent,
To liberate, to elevate,
In every breath, the self eludes.

Inhale courage, exhale fear,
Deep breathing's whispers, crystal clear,
In rhythm's dance, find harmony,
Aligning power, spirit's key.

Strength flows in the breath's embrace,
Deepening roots in timeless space,
Aligned with power, spirit's flight,
In breath's rhythm, find the might.

Song of the Breath: Melodies in Life's Rhythm

Breathing defines the melody,
In life's symphony, it's the key,
Inhale the passion, exhale the strife,
In each breath, the essence of life.

Defining the rhythm, a pulse so clear,
Inhale the joy, exhale the fear,
The song of life in every breath,
Harmony found in life and death.

Each inhalation, a new beginning,
Exhalation, release, no sinning,
Rhythm of breathing, song of the heart,
In each beat, a fresh start.

Listen closely, to the breath's song,
In its rhythm, where you belong,
Breathing in harmony, with the flow,
In the melody of life, let love grow.

Echoes of Harmony: Healing through Sound

In the silence where echoes dwell,
Sound healing's tale, it does tell,
Reverberations, soft and deep,
Echoes of peace, where souls do keep.

Harmonies dance, in waves they flow,
Touching places, we didn't know,
Sound vibrations, healing deep,
Echoes of peace, in silence keep.

Melodies weave, in patterns vast,
Echoes of peace, from future past,
In each reverberation, find,
Healing echoes, to unwind.

In echoes of sound, let healing flow,
Touching hearts, where dreams grow,
In every chord, in every tone,
Echoes of sound, we are not alone.

Whispers of the Serene Sky: A Journey through Tranquil Horizons

On the shore where waves caress,
The sands of time, a soft address,
A lullaby of ocean's grace,
Brings calm to hearts, a sacred space.

No ripples in the tranquil stream,
Just the soft embrace of a dream,
Where worries fade and troubles cease,
In the gentle arms of peace.

No storms to cloud the azure sky,
Just the gentle seabirds' cry,
In the symphony of the sea,
A peaceful mind is wild and free.

With every ebb and flow of tide,
A whisper from the deep inside,
Guides us to that tranquil place,
Where calm and peace, we embrace.

Vibrations of the Divine: Energy and Sound in Spiritual Awakening

Echoes of sound, soft and profound,
Healing vibrations all around,
Energy stirs, within the core,
Awakening spirits to explore.

Harmony flows, in waves of light,
Guiding souls through the darkest night,
Awakening whispers, soft and pure,
In sound's embrace, find the cure.

Each note a whisper, each tone a key,
Unlocking realms where spirits see,
The path to awakening, clear and true,
Sound's healing power, ever new.

In every note, a spark of grace,
Sound and energy, interlace,
Spiritual awakening, gentle and bright,
Guided by sound, embraced by light.

Infinite Horizons: A Spiritual Passage through Space

Beyond the realm of time and space,
Where stars in endless patterns trace,
A spiritual crossing, pure and free,
The universe calls, and soars the key.

Through the veil of time it flies,
Among the planets, through the skies,
A journey deep, a quest so pure,
In the cosmos, spirits endure.

Eclipses dance in shadow play,
Comets blaze, then fade away,
In this crossing, wisdom flows,
In the universe, the spirit grows.

Harmony in the stars' embrace,
A journey to the sacred place,
In the vast expanse, the soul will find,
The universe, forever aligned.

Emerald Glow: The Awakening Heart Chakra

In the heart's sacred space, a dance begins,
As the heart chakra opens, love within,
Radiant green, a gentle hue,
Connecting spirits, old and new.

Green emerald light, softly shines,
In the heart chakra's sacred lines,
Healing wounds, of past and pain,
Embracing love, once again.

Embrace of compassion, so deep,
In the heart's center, secrets keep,
Forgiveness whispers, in each beat,
Healing wounds, where love's complete.

In each heartbeat, a sacred song,
In the heart chakra, where we belong,
Opening wide, to love's embrace,
In the heart's journey, find your place.

Wisdom's Halo: The Journey through the Crown Chakra

Atop the head, where wisdom lies,
The Crown Chakra opens wide,
A portal to the cosmic sea,
Where spirit soars, and souls are free.

Lotus blooms, in thousand fold,
In the Crown Chakra, stories told,
Wisdom flows, like river's bend,
In the Crown Chakra, journey's end.

Celestial whispers, in ethereal air,
In the Crown Chakra, truths declare,
Divine guidance, in gentle sway,
In the Crown Chakra, find your way.

Silent whispers, in cosmic breeze,
Awakening souls, with gentle ease,
In the Crown Chakra's timeless space,
Find serenity, find grace.

Vital Force: Harnessing the Power Inside

Beneath the skin, where veins entwine,
Lies the power, so divine,
Pulses race, in rhythmic flow,
Power inside, begins to grow.

In the mind, where thoughts ignite,
Power inside, in every fight,
Strength in silence, courage found,
Power inside, forever bound.

In times of strife, it stands its ground,
The power inside, forever found,
Strength in bones, and marrow deep,
Power inside, the spirit will keep.

In the body, a fortress strong,
Power inside, where it belongs,
Endurance tested, and spirits soar,
Power inside, forevermore.

Spiritual Resonance: Exploring Core Energy Within

Within the vessel, where life resides,
Core energy, in currents glide,
Vitality surges, in every vein,
Life within, a cosmic refrain.

From the depths of marrow's hold,
To the spirit's stories, yet untold,
Core energy pulses, strong and true,
Life's essence, in all we do.

In the bones, where strength is found,
Core energy, a steady ground,
Life's journey, through the unknown,
In the body's core, life's throne.

In the silence of the night,
Core energy, a guiding light,
Life's essence, in each desire,
Burning bright, like eternal fire.

Fluttering Melodies: Butterflies Enlighten

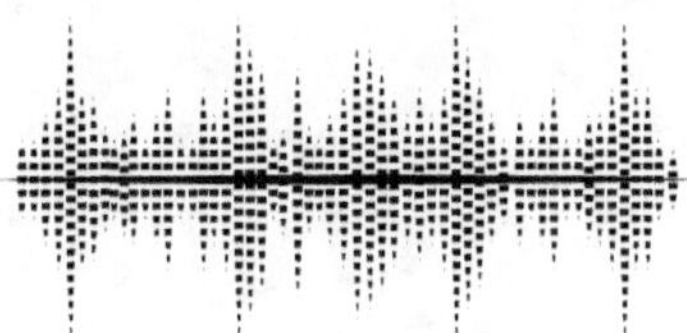

From cocoons of silence, they emerge,
Butterflies with wings that surge,
Each a story, a journey unfurled,
Symphony of butterflies, enlighten the world.

With fragile wings, they journey far,
A dance of freedom, beneath the stars,
Their silent flight, a song so pure,
Enlightening souls, forevermore.

Transformed by light, in colors bold,
They whisper secrets, never told,
Fluttering dreams, in patterns swirled,
Symphony of butterflies, a sacred world.

Their flight a dance, in air so clear,
Their essence whispers, "have no fear",
Enlightening souls, where dreams are curled,
Symphony of butterflies, in grace unfurled.

Transcendence Within: Transformation's Impact on Inner Capabilities

From seed to bloom, a journey unfolds,
Transformation's tale, in petals of gold,
Nurturing potential, in soil so deep,
Inner capabilities, awaken from sleep.

From bud to blossom, the heart's true call,
Transformation echoes, as barriers fall,
Stretching towards the sun's warm embrace,
Developing essence, in grace and pace.

Inner capabilities, like petals unfurled,
In transformation's embrace, wisdom swirled,
From doubt to courage, from fear to flight,
Developing strength, in the journey's light.

Embrace the chrysalis, where shadows reside,
Transforming limitations, to strength that strides,
Unlocking potential, like a hidden treasure,
Inner capabilities, in full measure.

Manifesting Miracles: Fulfilling Dreams with Faith and Action

In the dance of destiny's embrace,
Manifestation finds its place,
Whispers of possibility, in every gleam,
Fulfilling dreams, beyond the dream.

From seed to sprout, in fertile soil,
Manifestation, as dreams uncoil,
Watered by faith, and nurtured by love,
Fulfilling dreams, in the skies above.

In the symphony of life's grand score,
Manifestation opens every door,
Opportunity beckons, with a gentle beam,
Fulfilling dreams, in the dreamer's dream.

With each intention, a seed is sown,
Manifestation, in dreams unknown,
Through trials faced, and victories won,
Fulfilling dreams, beneath the sun.

Shine Bright: Developing Your Positive Aura

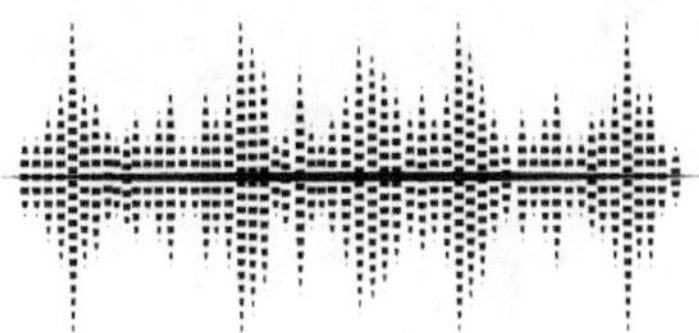

In the essence of being, where spirits soar,
A positive aura, forevermore,
In every thought, in every deed,
A positive aura, plants the seed.

From negativity, it turns away,
A positive aura, lights the way,
In darkness' grip, it shines bright,
Guiding hearts, through the night.

Through mindfulness' art, and courage's call,
A positive aura, stands tall,
In every breath, in every sigh,
A positive aura, lifts high.

In the dance of joy, and sorrow's pain,
A positive aura, remains, steadfast, sane,
Through storms that rage, and skies that clear,
Every moment, it is near.

Quiet Reflections: Nurturing Peaceful Aura

In the symphony of silence's song,
Aura of peace, where hearts belong,
Harmony woven, in quiet refrain,
Generating calmness, amid life's strain.

From the chaos of the world's uproar,
Aura of peace, a peaceful shore,
In the heart's haven, where troubles cease,
Generating calmness, in inner peace.

In the hush of twilight's embrace,
Aura of peace, finds its place,
Softly glowing, like moonlit beams,
Generating calmness, in silent dreams.

In the depths of the soul's retreat,
Aura of peace, finds its beat,
Echoes of tranquillity, in every breath,
Calmness reigns, banishing death.

Soulful Gaze: Reaching the Essence Within

In the dance of shadows, and light's caress,
Reflection of soul, in tenderness,
Essence unveiled, in each reflection's gleam,
Generating power, in life's grand scheme.

Ripples dance, in gentle sway,
Reflection of soul, in light's array,
Echoes of dreams, in waters deep,
Reaching the soul, in secrets keep.

Through valleys deep, and mountains high,
Reflection of soul, against the sky,
Strength emerges, in shadows cast,
Generating power, to break free at last.

Through reflections clear, and echoes old,
Reflection of soul, in stories told,
In every moment, whole and true,
Reaching the soul, where dreams pursue.

Spiritual Continuity: Mind and Soul in Consistency

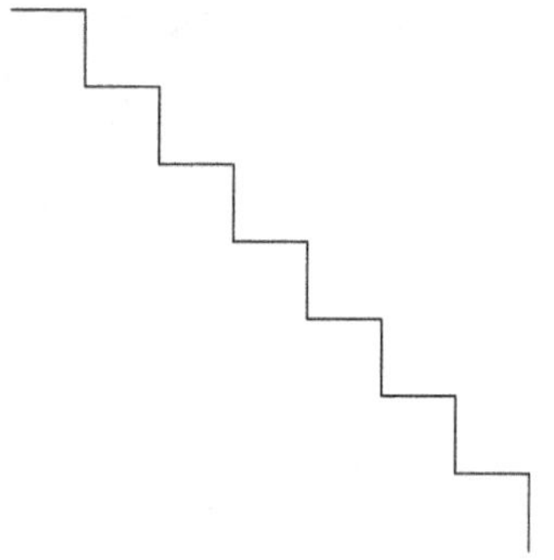

In the dance of stars, and moon's soft glow,
Consistency binds, in ebb and flow,
A unity found, where dreams aspire,
Connecting mind and soul, in fire.

Mind's clarity, in soul's embrace,
Consistency found, in silent grace,
In each breath taken, a rhythm's beat,
Connecting mind and soul, in complete.

In the symphony of nature's grace,
Consistency found, in every place,
From dawn's first light, to twilight's hue,
Connecting mind and soul, in view.

Through trials faced, and victories won,
Consistency's journey, never undone,
In every moment, where dreams unfurl,
Mind and soul, in harmony, swirl.

Destiny's Call: Seeking the Path Within

In the silence of the soul's retreat,
Seeking the path, where truths meet,
Believing in the life's true call,
Where echoes of destiny softly fall.

Through mists of doubt, and storms that brew,
Seeking the path, where skies are blue,
In every heartache, resilience found,
Believing in life, profound.

In whispers of the wind's soft sigh,
Seeking the path where eagles fly,
In every step, courage found,
Believing in life unbound.

Through shadows cast, and light's embrace,
Seeking the path, with steadfast grace,
In every breath, a spirit free,
Believing in life, to be.

Purposeful Presence: Creating an Aura of Influence

The purpose unfolds, like threads of gold,
To create an aura, brave and bold,
In every heartbeat, destiny's call,
Realming circumstances, standing tall.

With every heartbeat, a rhythm's beat,
The purpose whispers, in life's retreat,
A gentle aura, in every hue,
Realming circumstances, in skies so blue.

In the dance of stars, and moon's soft glow,
The purpose weaves, in ebb and flow,
In every heartbeat, a story told,
Realming circumstances, in souls bold.

With every breath, a spirit's sigh,
The purpose whispers, never shy,
In every soul's journey, a tale untold,
Realming circumstances, in stories bold.

Echoes of Identity: Journeying Within

On the canvas of life's grand design,
I paint the colors, so divine,
A journey to self, in shades so bright,
Embracing identity, in the light.

In the depths where shadows lie,
I search for answers, asking why,
In silence found, a whispering call,
Echoes of myself, standing tall.

With every dawn, a new beginning,
A journey to the self, in light winning,
In every stride, courage found,
Unveiling mysteries, profound.

In the symphony of heart's embrace,
I find myself, in a sacred space,
In every breath, a soul's embrace,
A journey to self, in grace.

Whispers of Perfume: Guiding the Spiritual Journey

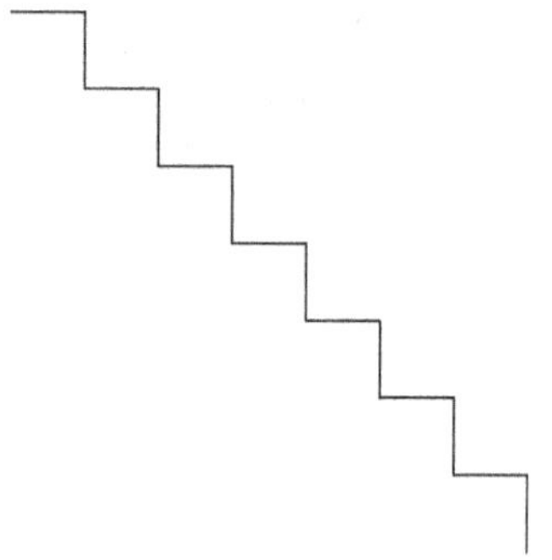

On the path of spirituality's rise,
Perfume's essence, a soothing guise,
In every step, a fragrance rare,
Enlightening the path, beyond comparison.

Through echoes of time's refrain,
Perfume's essence, in gentle rain,
In every breath, a sacred dance,
Enlightening the path, in the soul's trance.

With every bloom, a scent divine,
Perfume's essence, in moonlit shine,
In every sigh, a fragrance true,
Enlightening the path, in hues of blue.

In the garden of the soul's retreat,
Perfume's essence, in petals sweet,
In every moment, a touch sublime,
Enlightening the path, in endless time.

Sacred Steps: Following the Divine Pathway

On the quest for truth's embrace,
Destiny beckons, in sacred space,
A journey divine, in paths unknown,
Eternal quest, where seeds are sown.

Through valleys deep, and mountains high,
Divine path leads, beneath the sky,
In every tear shed, and joyous cry,
Destiny's journey, where dreams fly.

With every sunrise, a new day's dawn,
Divine path leads, where hope is drawn,
In every challenge, strength prevails,
Destiny's course, in wind and sails.

Through mists of time, and trials untold,
Divine path leads, in stories bold,
In every soul's journey, a tale to tell,
Destiny's path, where spirits dwell.

Shining Pathways: Discovering Life's Light

In the silence of the soul's embrace,
Illuminating light, finds its place,
A glow that warms the coldest night,
Revealing truths, in gentle light.

Through shadows cast and fears untold,
Illuminating light, so bold,
In every heart, a spark ignites,
Guiding paths through darkest nights.

With each day's end, a twilight's gleam,
Illuminating light, in evening's dream,
In every star that dots the sky,
To guide us home, where dreams fly.

In the symphony of heart's sweet song,
Illuminating light, where souls belong,
In every journey, a purpose found,
To illuminate life, all around.

Cosmic Connections: Where Science Meets Spirituality

In waves that ripple through the mind,
Science and spirituality entwined,
In quantum realms where particles play,
Uncertainty and wonder sway.

Yet in the quiet of a meditative hour,
Spirituality seeks its power,
In the unity of all that's known,
Where science and spirit have grown.

Yet in the silence that atoms weave,
Spirituality finds reprieve,
A connection in the unseen thread,
Where science and soul are wed.

For in the atoms that we trace,
Spirituality finds its place,
A universe within our grasp,
Where science and spirit clasp.

Songs of Enlightenment: Awakening the Soul's Song

In the echoes of eternity's expanse,
The soul's song weaves its tender dance,
Through echoes of past and dreams untold,
A melody of silver and gold.

In every heartbeat's steady thrum,
The soul's song hums, where dreams become,
In every laughter and every tear,
A song of courage, without fear.

With each heartbeat, a rhythmic beat,
The soul's song finds its own retreat,
In harmonies that lift and console,
A chorus that heals, making whole.

For in the quiet of the night's embrace,
The soul's song finds its sacred place,
A melody that transcends the mind,
A song of peace, forever kind.

Chanting the Soul Awake: Unlocking Inner Power

In the cadence of each chant,
Lies the power to enchant,
A melody of ancient lore,
Strengthening the core once more.

With each mantra, a step anew,
Inner strength, to see things through,
In every breath, a mantra's call,
Chanting echoes, standing tall.

In the silence, in the hush,
Chanting weaves a tranquil brush,
Threads of courage, threads of light,
Reignite the soul's inner might.

Chanting is the key, they say,
To unlock the dawn of the day,
Where shadows fade and spirits soar,
Inner strength forevermore.

Divine Clarity: Nurturing the Rays of Enlightenment

In the dance of stars that paint the night,
Rays of enlightenment, shine bright,
Across the canvas of endless space,
Echoes of eternity, embrace.

Through galaxies that spiral and spin,
Rays of enlightenment, dwell within,
In the quiet of cosmic symphony,
Harmony found in unity.

With each constellation's gentle gleam,
Rays of enlightenment, dreams redeem,
In the silence of the universe's call,
Whispers of wisdom, for one and all.

For in the cosmic dance's flow,
Rays of enlightenment, wisdom grow,
Connecting hearts, across the skies,
To infinite truths, where spirit flies.

Midnight Dance: Mystical Steps Beneath the Moon

Beneath the silver veil of night,
Where stars embroider velvet sky,
We dance upon the meadow's grace,
In moonlit waltz, a gentle pace.

The moon, a lantern in the sky,
Casting magic, we can't deny,
We move in circles, hand in hand,
In moonlit trance, where spirits stand.

Each movement tells a silent tale,
Serenade of shadows, hearts prevail,
In moonlit serenade, we find,
Our souls entwined, in a lunar bind.

For in this dance, our spirits blend,
Serenade of shadows, without end,
In moonlit trance, we find our tune,
Dancing beneath the silver moon.

Unity in Motion: Dance for Global Peace

Dance for peace, with steps so light,
In circles wide, in shadows bright,
With hearts aligned and spirits free,
We sway and spin, in unity.

Dance for peace, in joy and pain,
In windswept fields, in pouring rain,
In unity, we find our voice,
To make a world where all rejoice.

For peace is more than just a word,
It's in the steps, the songs we've heard,
In this dance, we take a stand,
To spread peace across the land.

Dance for peace, with passion true,
In each embrace, a world anew,
Where conflicts fade, and hearts release,
In this dance, we find our peace.

Divine Mercy: In the Grace of God

In the grace of God, I spread my wings,
To soar above life's fleeting things,
In His embrace, I find my flight,
Guided by His loving light.

Through valleys low and mountains high,
In the grace of God, I testify,
Of His mercy, of His grace,
Sustaining me in every place.

In the dance of life, in the stormy sea,
In the grace of God, He carries me,
To shores of peace, to lands unknown,
In His grace, I'm never alone.

For in His grace, I find my way,
In His grace, I kneel and pray,
To live my life, to walk this sod,
Forever blessed, in the grace of God.

Divine Caress: Embracing Earth's Splendor

Upon the Earth, where wildflowers bloom,
Kissing the Earth with their vibrant plume,
Petals soft, like whispers of the wind,
Embracing the Earth, where life begins.

In fields of green, under azure skies,
Kissing the Earth, where beauty lies,
Each blade of grass, each leaf that sways,
A symphony of life's displays.

The sun, a kiss upon the land,
Kissing the Earth with its golden hand,
A gentle touch, a warm caress,
Blessing the Earth with tenderness.

For in this dance of light and shade,
Kissing the Earth, where dreams are made,
We find in nature's tapestry,
The beauty of life, eternally.

Sacred Portal: A Gateway to Spiritual Awakening

At dawn's first light, the portal gleams,
A threshold of light, where dreams,
Take flight upon the wings of grace,
Divine portal, in sacred space.

Through the veil, where mysteries unfold,
Divine portal, where stories told,
Of love and wisdom, boundless and true,
Guiding us to what is due.

In the silence of the soul's embrace,
Divine portal, in timeless grace,
A passage to realms unknown,
Where seeds of faith and hope are sown.

For in this portal, hearts unite,
In love's embrace, in purest light,
To journey forth, beyond the veil,
Divine portal, where truths prevail.

Echoes of Shivohum: Awakening the Soul

In the chant of ancient hymn,
Shivohum, the soul within,
Awakens to the sacred fire,
Of Shiva's grace, divine desire.

Through the cycles of birth and death,
Shivohum, the eternal breath,
I am the silence, I am the storm,
In Shivohum, my spirit is reborn.

In the temple of my beating heart,
Shivohum, where worlds apart,
Merge in union, in sacred rhyme,
Shivohum, through endless time.

For in this mantra's sacred call,
Shivohum, I rise and fall,
In Shiva's dance, I find my home,
In Shivohum, I am Shiva, I am one.

Grateful Whispers: Finding Peace in the Spiritual Path

On the wings of time, I soar,
Gratitude, forevermore,
For every sunrise, for every star,
Gratitude, that fills my heart.

In the echoes of the spirit's call,
Gratitude, standing tall,
For every friend, for every foe,
Gratitude, that helps me grow.

In the dance of seasons' change,
Gratitude, that rearrange,
My thoughts, my fears, my dreams, my heart,
Gratitude, my counterpart.

For every blessing, great or small,
Gratitude, I give my all,
To the journey, with every part,
Gratitude, the soul's true art.